Abc

Yash is a poet with a deep love for the written word. Inspired by the beauty of life's intricacies, his verses dance with emotion and vivid imagery. Drawing from a palette of art, music, and the flavors of the world, Yash weaves a tapestry of poetic expression that captures the essence of the human experience. With his pen as his brush and his heart as his guide, Yash invites readers on a journey through the magic of his words, exploring the depths of emotions and savoring the joy of existence.

THEN, COME BACK TO YOURSELF

Yash Shah

THEN, COME BACK TO YOURSELF

Edited by Sameen Umar

Vanguard Press

VANGUARD PAPERBACK

© Copyright 2024
Yash Shah

The right of Yash Shah to be identified as author of this work has been asserted by him in accordance with the Copyright, Designs and Patents Act 1988.

All Rights Reserved

No reproduction, copy or transmission of this publication may be made without written permission.
No paragraph of this publication may be reproduced, copied or transmitted save with the written permission of the publisher, or in accordance with the provisions of the Copyright Act 1956 (as amended).

Any person who commits any unauthorised act in relation to this publication may be liable to criminal prosecution and civil claims for damages.

A CIP catalogue record for this title is available from the British Library.

ISBN 978-1-83794-218-3
This is a work of fiction. Names, characters, businesses, places, events and incidents are either the products of the author's imagination or used in a fictitious manner. Any resemblance to actual persons, living or dead, or actual events is purely coincidental.

Vanguard Press is an imprint of
Pegasus Elliot Mackenzie Publishers Ltd.
www.pegasuspublishers.com

First Published in 2024

**Vanguard Press
Sheraton House Castle Park
Cambridge England**

Printed & Bound in Great Britain

Dedication

To nature and life. To everyone around me. You have always been my unwavering source of inspiration, guiding lights in my life, and pillars of support. This book is a heartfelt tribute to the love and belief you have showered upon me. Thank you for being my rock, my muse, and my everything. Without your presence and encouragement, these poems would not have been possible.

Acknowledgements

I would like to express my heartfelt gratitude to the following individuals and organizations who have contributed to the creation and publication of this poetry book: My sincere thanks to my family, especially my spouse, parents, and sibling, for their unwavering love, encouragement, and belief in my writing. Your constant support has been invaluable. I am deeply grateful to my friends who have been a source of inspiration and have provided valuable feedback on my poems. Your enthusiasm and honest critiques have helped shape this collection. A special thank you to Kruti and Sameen, whose insightful discussions and constructive criticism have significantly influenced my growth as a poet. Your encouragement and camaraderie have been instrumental in this journey. I am deeply grateful to my friends, Ayushi and Kena, for their exceptional artistic talents and the beautiful illustrations they have provided for this book. Your creative contributions have brought an added layer of beauty and meaning to my poems. I extend my appreciation to my mentors and teachers, both past and present, for their guidance, wisdom, and invaluable lessons. Your expertise and passion for the written word have shaped my artistic voice I would also like to acknowledge the publishing team at Pegasus and professionals who have worked tirelessly to bring this book to life. Your dedication and expertise in editing, design, and production have transformed my words into a tangible creation. Lastly, I am grateful to the readers and poetry enthusiasts who have embraced and supported my work. Your engagement and encouragement fuel my creative spirit. Thank you all for being a part of this poetic adventure. Your contributions have made this book possible, and I am truly grateful for your presence in my life.

1.

As I watch a sunset,
The orange and yellow hues,
the only thought that becomes apparent,
Is the magnificent view.
The moment breaks as a bird flies by,
Wings fluttering to stay afloat,
Creating a beautifully tortured breeze.
Unblinking, a thought makes itself known as I watch the white movement.
Can I fly too?
I watch the little creature sail the unseen drafts until not even a dot remains to the eye.
And yet, the adoration remains as prominent as the sun in the sky.
Adoration for the weightless being
Gliding parallel between the earth and sky,
Able to pick its destination,
Bound by no such thing as meager as gravity.
Alone once again, I look to the sky
The mix of the colors and hope to fly.

2.

In the violent winds of truth,
In the burnt smell of broken trust,
In the paralyzing fear of losing,
I found humanity.

In the soft touch of rain,
In the petrichor fragrance of sand,
In the harmonizing melody of the earth,
I found the meaning of living.

3.

I wonder,
how can I leave all this behind?
The stress in the act of being here,
so entirely encompassing.
Do I think about it too much?
Do I think about it enough?
Maybe, I'm trying to find something lost,
Maybe, I am the one who is lost.
I start walking, no path in mind.
A fog in my head,
A whirlwind of thoughts,
Yet so entirely void.
People I care about?
Things I care for?
Everything?
Anything?
An answer is all I want.
There!
I can see it in the distance,
But the closer I get,
the further it drifts.

4.

The changing colors of a leaf,
always make me believe.
Believe that a change is all I need,
All I need for a heartache's relief.

5.

You know, there are people in your life
Who stayed by your side, maybe for no reason
But you never noticed, too busy in strife
For someone who turned out to be a mere season

6.

I'll catch fire and risk the burn,
To finish this chapter and the next in turn,
They said walk, but I chose to run,
Filled up my tank, taking the next turn,
Bruises remain, a lesson learned,
But I won't hesitate and miss what's to be earned.

7.

Ask yourself, are you truly asking yourself?
It's been so long since you've cracked a smile
Perhaps you're waiting for greater things to arrive
Open your eyes and gaze outside
See how the sun rises and shines.
It needs no help to brighten up our skies
Maybe it's you, you're the one thing
That can make you feel alive
Don't cry, it's just a moment in time
Now it's your chance to shine.

8.

Only the moon can glow from the shine of the sun,
I would make the most of every opportunity;
Than to have none.

9.

I did not ask you before loving you.
Why should I ask now?
I just want to stay here by your side,
After all that we've been through.

I was lost in my mind,
Yet you took care of my heart.
I was lost in my mind,
Yet you gently guarded my soul.

There's no end to this winding path,
So by your side I'll stay.
Until you no longer want me,
Forever, I will stay.

10.

I will get through this,
I've done it time and time again.
Sometimes the cost is mine to bear,
Sometimes I pay for someone else.

11.

I sat down to remember the talks I had with myself from years ago,
Just to find out, they were so fresh, I'd had them mere moments ago.

12.

Both mind and heart are divided into two different cages,
My diary is full of so many crumpled and empty pages.
I listen to one, often more than the other,
As I navigate this life full of twists and turns,
I wonder which one I should trust to lead me to the right outcome.

The mind, with its rationality and logic, often seems like the safer choice,
But the heart, with its boundless compassion and empathy, holds a certain poise.
Both are necessary, and both are valid in their own ways,
Yet still, I struggle to find the balance between the two every day.

For how can one decide which path to take,
When both the heart and mind offer their own reasons and stakes?
In the end, it is up to me to make the choice,
To follow my head or my heart and let it be my guiding voice.

13.

There is a melody everywhere,
Rhythmically healing my heart with its care.
It has become my dearest friend,
Singing its deepest secrets without end.
Through its song every moment of the day,
It brings me warmth and undying rest, come what may.

I always believe in it,
In its unspoken chorus and verse, a perfect fit,
As it never leaves my heart untouched,
Bringing out feelings I didn't know I had in me and such.

I often listen to its accompanying harmony,
An enchanting tune that sets my spirit free,
And I know I'll forever need it, but I also know,
That there will be a day of silence, as someone else will need its song to grow.

For this melody is a gift to be shared,
Spreading joy and comfort wherever it's aired,
And though it may depart from my ears,
Its beauty and healing will always persevere.

14.

Words.
Can't save yourself
from their bruises, cuts, and tears
they stay with you, haunting
like unwelcome fears

Words.
Go away.
Memories, stay
let it rain and let me cry
let it shine and let me dry
for every tear that falls
a part within me calls

Words.
Let me be, the more I remember
the more I'm back and the more I'm there
the more I can't bear, but I'll try
to face the pain and not deny

For in the end, it's through the hurt
that we learn to heal and grow
and though it's hard, we can't avert
the path that we must go

So, let it rain and let me cry

let it shine and let me dry
for with each step I take
I become stronger, and not break.

15.

Screaming, but no one hears me anymore,
Breaking glass against the floor,
The shards run red by my feet,
Nothing feels right anymore.

Lost and drowning in my despair,
My heart feels heavy, my soul is bare,
I try to reach out, but no one seems to care,
Alone and lost, I'm beyond repair.

But I can't give up, I must take control,
Rise from the ashes, and fight for my goal,
Though my wounds are deep, and my scars still show,
I'll keep moving forward, and never let go.

So I'll scream even louder, until I'm heard,
Pick up the broken pieces, and let go of the hurt,
Find the strength within, to rise from the dirt,
And build myself back up, stronger and assertive.

With each step I take, I'll leave the past behind,
And though the road ahead may be unkind,
I'll stand tall and strong, with a clear mind,
And overcome every obstacle that I may find.

16.

Death can be beautiful.
Let your ego die.
Embrace humility with grace.
That's when your pride will come alive.

17.

Though life has been gracious,
It won't always be each time,
Let this moment be grateful,
Like your heart and mind.

For your heart knows the way,
Your smile know joy and pain,
With each inhale you take,
You can soar to the sky again.

Embrace the gratitude,
Let it fill your soul.
In each moment of life,
There's beauty yet to behold.

Let the sunshine caress your face,
Let the breeze tickle your skin.
Know that every step you take,
Is a chance to begin again.

So, breathe in deep, my friend,
And let your spirit fly,
For with each inhale you take,
You can touch the sky so high.

18.

With your head on my shoulder,
We led and followed in perfect rhyme,
My heart needed a mirror,
So, I looked at you, and saw myself shine.

But now when I gaze into your eyes,
I see more than just a reflection,
I see the depth of your soul, your spirit,
The intense vibrance of your affection.

Like a horizon, we rise and drown,
In the sea of our love and emotion,
New and greater heights open,
Ones that show no descent of devotion.

Let our hearts be intertwined,
In a dance of joy and bliss,
For with you by my side, my love,
I know that life is not to be missed.

And though we may have our highs and lows,
Ups and downs due to the sands of time.
Our love will always lift us up,
And guide us to a place sublime.

19.

My heart spoke and I believed in it.
Falling was the only way to realize no arms would hold me.
I have to find my own way,
Land on my own feet.

I was fooled by my own desires,
The urges for the gaps to be filled.
They were just illusions,
Ones created to escape the fear,
To fill my own need.

20.

Accept that one flaw in your body,
One you thought no one would accept.

Accept that move in your dance,
The one that makes you burst out and laugh.

Accept the birthmark.
Accept your past.

Who will love you if you yourself can't?

In a garden full of flowers,
Accept the leaf.
The one that lost its colour,
But still attracted the lark.

21.

In presenting its own truth,
Mirrors were hurt by their own hand.
Unseeing cracks formed a web,
Similar to that of a handprint.

The broken can still be fixed.
The wound spilling the river of life can be mended.
If the selfish desires leave,
He can be set free from the confines of his greed.

22.

Without purpose, life is like a seed,
Waiting to bloom into something more,

But to grow into a strong tree indeed,
It needs to know what its roots are for.

23

With my guitar in my hand,
I wait to play a song for myself,
But sometimes the rhythm makes me stand,
On a road that seems to stretch endlessly.

I wonder if I'll hit a wrong note,
Or if I'll find the right chord,
But then I remind myself to devote,
To the music and not the discord.

24.

Colors of the rainbow, more than seven I see,
A palette of hues, waiting for me.

The more I achieve, the more I want to run,
A passion within, that cannot be undone.

This must be it, this must be my compulsion,
A drive to succeed, to avoid the convulsion.

Colors of the rainbow, a symbol of my quest,
A journey of discovery, one that never rests.

So I'll chase my dreams, with passion and zeal,
And embrace each moment, with the hope to reveal,

The beauty of life, in its many hues,
A rainbow of possibilities, for me to choose.

25.

It didn't matter how I won.
At least for those who didn't watch, for those who shunned.
It didn't matter to those who didn't care.

It didn't matter if the bullet hit me.
Showcasing the decision of bravery to save the people behind me.
It didn't matter that I didn't dodge.

26.

Wind humming its tune by my ears,
Accelerating the sadness and encouraging my tears.

It all happened so sudden and so acute,
My heart missed a beat to scream;
Only for my mouth to remain mute.

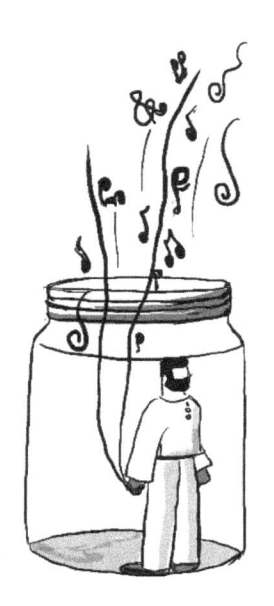

I wondered how I'd bear all this rage
Out of control; burning soul
The bird remained encompassed in its nest,
Never leaving its self-built cage.

27.

I kept my heart clean
like the clearest of waters
My mind threw dirt at me
replacing a crystal spring with a swamp
it was just a start,
looking into the mirror,
A pebble making a motion in a void of stillness
The water turned from a spring
Into a raging ocean of self-hatred
God, please help me.
Give me the strength to be set free
I'll always remember the dirt trickling into the sea
My mind is still hurting,
but at the very least,
It's free.

28.

You know it's hard
to understand the concept of self-love

It's like fighting a war with yourself
a war where you have to fly a dove

I'm urban, I'm modern
on the top of that I don't surrender

it's always changing, I'm always growing
outside I'm tired, inside I'm dying

everyday I'm running, aiming for flying
I get that, I need that and so is crying

I have to stop, I have to breathe and I will glow
for the first time I think I'm someone,
someone I want to know.

29.

Amidst a world full of vibrant hues,
I live my life in black and white.
Always preparing for tomorrow,
While losing the light of today.

The more I look above the horizon,
The more I begin to see.
Even as the raindrops fall,
There's still time left for me.

For in the darkness of the storm,
A rainbow's colors can appear,
A reminder that in life's struggles,
There's always something to revere.

30.

My heart beats fast and my thoughts spin wild each time I think of her smile.
Her beauty shines, telling me no,
I'm not good enough to hold her close.

Yet,
I stop to look within.
I realize,
The me now is better than what I've ever been.
I'll love myself and stay this way still.
With or without her,
My heart will always be filled.

I'll be vulnerable and take a chance,
Maybe I'll even learn to dance.
For now I love myself and in this way,
I'll love her fully too,
Come what may.

So even if she never sees the love I keep inside of me,
My heart will keep loving strong and true,
For me,
For her,
For everything that's new.

31.

They say that someday,
The skies will clear.
And all the chaos and confusion,
Will inevitably disappear.

Until that day arrives,
I'll hold on tight.
I'll keep weathering the storm
With all my might.

Though the road ahead is long and filled with stops and turns,
I'll keep on moving forward with a spirit that is unbroken and undeterred.

32.

Why should my happiness
be dependent on you?
Why should I wake up
to find out the dream isn't true?

Did I give you my permission to rely on you?
Or did you assume that these feelings I have can also be
played with by you?

For this mystery,
I've finally gotten the clue.
Broken dreams cannot be fixed,
With any guilt or glue.

I should have seen it when the sky no longer looked blue.
I would have stopped my feelings,
Before everything I put myself through.

33.

Remembering is agony
wisely having insanity
left you with cursed vanity.

34.

Today I stopped at the crossing again,
A fork in my direction leading me four ways.
I always choose the path on the right,
Afraid of what I might lose if I stray.

I'm scared to take the risk,
To venture away from my comfort zone.
I keep my feet safe in my shoes,
I keep myself safe in my routine.

I hope that God will make the right path known.
But what if the path that is less taken,
Is the path that leads to my dreams?
What if the risk is worth it?
What if it's not as bad as it seems?

So I take a deep breath and step forward,
Choosing a new path to explore,
I might stumble and fall along the way,
But I'll keep going,
Keep seeking for more.

35.

I want someone who truly wants me in their life.
My absence making itself known, making them feel
empty, like a starless sky

I won't disappoint them during their darkest nights,
I'll be their shadow in their brightest times.

This same trust I want them to have in me.
This is the same trust I need for myself,
So, I can be true to myself.

36.

Today, I'm lost and unsure
Uncertain of what I need to know, what I should endure

It feels like I'm an empty basket, filled with everyone's breath
Knowledge seeping in, but not the kind I think I need.

37.

You are your own hero, always battling
Don't believe the lies that you're not worth adding
To solve life's puzzles, we need every piece
Without you, this world's picture would never be complete.

Let your smile shine bright
The one you've kept hidden, with no love in sight
Or maybe it's just hiding somewhere below
But wherever it is, let it finally show.

38.

Ripping away a piece of my diary every day,
Bit by bit,
The memories fade away.

I write a new note for the song I want to play,
Yet, however frayed,
The notes of the old song stay strong in their sway.

39.

Empty roads hold so much more
You meet an eye, you can't ignore

The bittersweet feeling they provide
Of being lost and found, side by side

It contains so much for sure
Know that, even if you are, you are not alone.

40.

If I ever hear
someone else's heartbeat
in their silence,

It would be my sin
to watch them suffer
any violence

41.

Constantly I watch the water,
Never do I see it be the same.
Always changing when I look,
My reflection was made to be remade.

Each and every day I want to run,
That reflection in the water makes me come undone.
The guilt and the rage swirl inside me,
A chameleon is what the water should show me.

Each day I wish to run away,
But if a wish was all it took,
The reflection would stay the same.

I want to meet someone like me,
Someone whose company stops the raging breeze.
The wind stops when they are here,
And the reflection,
Finally becomes clear.

42.

Oh traveller, where will you take me?
Will it be here or there? Or somewhere that fits me?
Somewhere that it's free, somewhere it's meant to be.
Perhaps the sky above, or this land below
Something will kiss me.
I may feel fear but I know
You will always be with me

43.

Life, give me your best shot
A challenge I'll accept, a tie I couldn't knot

Provide me with your presence
When I forget your essence

This cold night won't stop me
Nor the extreme heat, I'll be

Life, I want to grow every day
Give me always a little more, I pray

44.

I cried out loud without yelling.
I complained to the world without a word being heard.
I cried on my pillow leaving it dry.
For how can I tell anyone anything,
When the world tells me,
Toughen up, there's no reason to cry!

45.

You may feel like giving up on gardening
Boredom setting in, it's no longer enchanting
But later on, you might be amazed
When you try farming, and the seeds you raised

For sometimes, the things that we think are mundane
Can blossom into beauty, like a flower in the rain
So don't be discouraged, keep pushing ahead
The best things in life often come from what we dread.

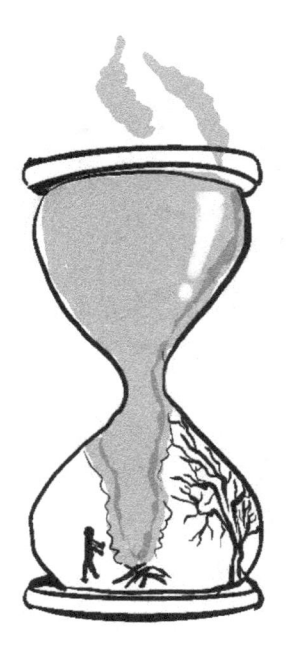

46.

You were always kind, even when you
Tried to kill your inner child, it's true.
You were always that kid, turned into a man
In the blink of an eye, you took a stand.

You were always brave, but sometimes scared,
Putting yourself in a cave, not knowing what's there.
But you emerged stronger, with a heart full of gold,
A story of triumph, one that deserves to be told.

47.

Keeping my eyes open, this wind brings tears.
Watching over everyone I care, but it only deepens my fears.

For every year that passes, I hurt myself more,
Carrying the weight of their pain, unsure.

But perhaps it's time to close my eyes,
To find my own peace, to my own surprise.

For I cannot save everyone, no matter how hard I try.
It's time to let go, to release the burden and fly.

48.

The passage of time brings the passing of pain,
As my loved ones depart once again.
This game that time plays,
I lose every single time.
For who can remain the same,
As time ticks away.

49.

Now every night I wake up
to a new wonderful daylight.

50.

Once there was a puppet,
With strings he held in his hand.
He controlled his own actions,
But mostly they were called bad.

Though he was alive on the outside,
Inside he was empty and dead.
If only he had known to cut the threads,
He could have freed himself instead.

51.

Peace is all over the place,
If you really want it to be found

Of course, there is a whole ocean of money out there,
What you really need is a pond.

52.

With a heart full of kindness
and eyes that see the best,
You bring light to the world
and leave others impressed.

53.

Don't worry if you choose
to quit and walk away,
For sometimes it's better
than on a wrong path to stay.

54.

Beneath the soil,
you grow stronger each day,
Absorbing pressure and stress,
Growing more confident in every way.

Like a seed planted deep,
You reach for the light,
Nurtured by the earth,
You blossom with all your might.

55.

What's wrong with an attitude that seeks to test,
Whether the ones who think less of you, truly do?
For too often we assume and let ourselves rest
On the perceptions of others, both false and true.

56.

Like always,
I burned my tongue again
Today, trying to have it all at once.
My drink was not cold enough,
And I was too impatient to wait.

Just like life,
When I tried to have it all at once,
I couldn't quite manage it.
My deeds weren't enough,
And my aspirations were too high.

57.

I barely see the flight
Of a thousand birds
In the wide blue ocean above me.
But when I do, I wish
To dive right into their freedom again.

I barely notice the foaming clouds,
And the therapeutic sound
Of peaceful waters below.
But when I do, I wish
To fly right into their tranquillity again.

58.

Nothing's ever enough
Nothing can be done for this heart to lock its door
someone always finds the key
or someone always is the key

59.

I am afraid
of the fear
that I have
about everything new.
Perhaps, it's not the newness itself
But it might be the thought of
letting the familiar go instead.

60.

With every step you take,
You show your will to thrive.
No obstacle can shake
The power you derive.

When life brings you pain,
Remember your strength within.
Calm your mind,
And let the healing begin.

61.

Making sense of what's lost
Its essence now alike
Politics and political jokes
Once meaningful, now adrift

I laugh at both with ease
For what else can I do
When truth is hard to seize
And lies are all too true

62.

These dreams you see,
Consciously and constantly,
Undoubtedly tell
Where you need to be.

What you need to see,
And that you need to hurry,
For time waits for no one,
And your destiny may flurry.

63.

Those invincible wings
of yours
is nothing but the gut
hidden beneath you

It sees the sky above
and afraid of what's under your feet
don't hold it, and never look down while reaching up

They didn't grow itself
nobody taught you how to jump high
It's you who's trying
It's you who's flying.

64.

Filling the pages, I write relaxed.
Yet when tomorrow comes,
Desire puts a pen in my hands.
I'm not sure when it'll end.
I'm stressed.
I'm trying to find reasons to stop the ink splash.
The colored water on my hand,
A reminder of the once innocent desire.

Now,
I look for peace.
Every day in the water,
I write a reflection of my thoughts.
I try to stop the secrets on paper,
But then I remember,
This diary,
Is part of the poetry.

65.

Do you feel as if this journey doesn't belong to you?

I might not see you,
But trust me,
This path is not the one meant for you.

This ride will have its ups and downs,
Will you ignore the signs?
Enjoy it while it lasts,
Memorize its turns and emotions.
It might be the best ride you have,
Compared to the next.

66.

A self-check, am I happy?
Why not, what's wrong today?
It's okay, tomorrow will be better,

With new chances to find your way.
You managed to breathe today,
And that's a victory to claim.

Tomorrow your smile will be greater,
And happiness won't be hard to sustain.

67.

Rough the wood may be,
But the leaves are soft and green.
Skin is just a wall,
What matters is the character within.

What's outside may be tough,
But inside we can be kind and serene.
Our true selves shine through,
For that's where beauty can be seen.

68.

Maybe everything's supposed to
be over
maybe that's why we mature
that's what we need, collection of memories

You will probably not remember me
for all the good that I did
maybe for all the bad
that I didn't let happen to you

So,
tell me if you need me
or not
I'll be here.

69.

How did you think
this hatred is worth it
it's not something that of course
will pause that relationship and cut it
it will push you from yourself
and break that bridge or maybe burn it.

70.

That's exactly what the second person is feeling right now,
A heart in turmoil, with no way to bow.
The weight of the world is heavy and strong,
And they wonder if they can go on for long.
The days go by, and the nights seem endless,
With no relief from the pain that is relentless.
They try to put on a brave face each day,
But deep down, they just want to run away.
They long for a ray of hope in the dark,
Something to cling to, a little spark.
But it seems like the light is out of reach,
And all they can do is silently beseech.
So they wait and hope for a change,
A little glimmer in their life to arrange.
And though it seems impossible right now,
They know they'll find a way to make it somehow.

71.

Oh rain,
drop of an angel
falling from the sky
in between those gaps
passing warm and bright
sunlight.
wonder how will it
look from its birth
till down from the top
each day
of the mountain
miles away from crowd

I am covered with
I am still thankful of my heart and mind
to be able to see the sky from inside this room, this wall,
and through the air that may came from some waterfall.

72.

Sometimes I bowed to those,
Who wanted me to stay down low,
I even prayed for those,
Who weren't aware when I followed their pain,
As they pioneered and led the way,
I trailed behind, hoping to learn and stay.
But now I stand tall and strong,
No longer bowing to those who did me wrong,
I've found my own path to follow,
No longer in the shadows, I can now glow.

73.

Why can't I see the way I did before?
Why can't I notice the small things anymore?

Cherishing the small details that brought love and warmth.
For who would see them in the first place,
Had they not been looking?

A memory of the pouring rain hitting stone,
Covering the lullaby of dull music lofting from the corner store.
I only see myself standing by the shore,
Where have you gone?
I want to know.

My heart doesn't beat for the small things anymore,
Is it because those little things don't seem to matter anymore?

74.

Oh, this pause,
this empty thoughts,
hope I don't become
meaningless words

Oh, this breaks,
what else will it take?
waking early morning,
everyday I'm still late.

Evening already,
this stress,
whatever I see, I eat,
such a disgrace.

Oh, this life,
can't live, can't leave,
I sleep tired,
woke up tired and peeve.

75.

Going away
I am running away
All the lies
Bizarre and those spotlights
I was giving myself.

76.

Pigeons, with wings so light,
Find their way to deliver messages right.
I receive thousands every day,
But wait for the one that's yet to find its way.
In the lost passages, I hope to meet,
The one who sends that message so sweet,
But the pigeons seem to have lost their way,
I wonder if they'll deliver their messages today.

77.

I saw hundreds of beautiful
Faces out there
The more I see smiles
The more I contemplate
Why I am not smiling, why I'm not happy?
No, oh no
Is it epicaricacy?

78.

For me
Karma would remember
The pain I see in your eyes,
Tears I see in those lashes.

Not that I laid that pain on you
I believe I am still
Part of the punishment

I didn't part your pain from you!

79.

You have been through all of it
All of the ends and all of the new beginnings
You know how much you cried
How much you can survive
You still have the courage
To learn and apply
Your bravery
Your slavery
It's time for you to untie.

80.

Wild wild thoughts
And let's not forget the dreams as well
Taking all from you
Nothing else is left in you
Your heart.

Will you give it some rest
will you sleep for a bit
Blank and empty
No emotions, no worries

81.

And another prayer has begun.
My entity is entitled for no one else
Isn't it obvious? We know the truth
We know whom to trust and we know
Whom should we not.
My feelings for taking care of me
My love for myself
And all this efforts I was giving to someone
in the end came back to me.

82.

My visions are not breathing
My dreams have become water
They vaporize when the sun hits my eyes
There's nothing I can remember
That I used to believe
It's new every time
Every day
Then I see pebbles
On my path
They are stopping me from diving
Into the ocean.

Why I am seeing beauty as a distraction
Is it you or me
Who's stopping me to look back at sky
Once again.

83.

My mind is like a raincloud,
Overflowing with thoughts galore,
Storms and thunders, waiting and wondering,
It bursts and lightens, then thinks some more.
Am I a good person, I ponder,
Will I help those who need me most?
But they can survive without me, can't they?
At what cost?
Is it my duty to humanity?
Oh no, my mind laughs and scoffs.
They don't need words
they don't understand words
they understand feelings
they understand killings.

84.

I believe in love,
A crashing wave against the rocks,
Relentless and persistent,
With each crash, it never stops.
But what role do I play,
In this eternal force of nature?
Like the wind, I'm swept away,
Lost in its mysterious allure.
All I know is I want to be,
Caught up in its tender embrace,
To love and be loved in return,
With a heart that beats with grace.
Why can't I feel the pain,
Of those shattered by love's might?
Before they're crushed and broken,
Reduced to dust in the night.

85.

Art can fix love between you and me,
It paints a picture that never dies.
A canvas of memories we hold so dear,
A masterpiece of moments, year after year.
Through brushstrokes and colors, we express,
Emotions that words can never impress.
The beauty of our love, forever preserved,
In a timeless work of art, undisturbed.
Whether it's a poem, a song, or a drawing,
Art captures the essence of our being.
It speaks to the heart, in ways we can't explain,
A bond between us, that will always remain.
So let's create our art, with passion and grace,
A tribute to our love, in every single place.
Let it be our legacy, for all the world to see,
That love and art can fix anything, you and me.

86.

The weight of my words,
Heavy on my mind,
As I try to express,
What's hard to define.
Half-formed thoughts escape,
But never make it through,
The barriers of my nerves,
My words so weak and few.
My heart remains incomplete,
Longing for release,
But my words fall short,
Leaving me in grief.
Life moves on so quickly,
As I try to catch the signs,
But my mind is unsure,
And my heart's mistakes, unkind.
I wish I could find the words,
To make my heart complete,
But until then, I'll keep trying,
To express what's hard to speak.

87.

Never-ending, this warm smell of the sun,
Along with the breeze and sometimes freshly cooked bread.
A coffee and a smile,
I once knew all these wonders and how they made my life happier.
I still danced and jumped in slow motion,
When music was perfect in my mind,
Making the perfect rhythm with my heart.
What has happened all so suddenly?
I am now concerned about all the little things,
Whether it's cavities or money,
And I don't touch ice cream, blaming both.
Have I grown up too fast?
I'm not sure.
Perhaps it's not me who's grown up too fast,
But other people who are rushing through life.
Maybe it's time to slow down,
And savor the little things that make life worth living.

88.

Another day weighed heavy like a stone,
Still and laden with a somber tone,
Until a flower caught my weary gaze,
Beside it, a butterfly danced and swayed.
Moved by the gentle caress of the air,
Their beauty intertwined, a sight so rare,
The blossom's colors and the butterfly's flight,
Enhanced each other with sheer delight.
In that moment, I couldn't help but smile,
As I witnessed nature's harmonious style.
I walked along, a wanderer, free and unbound,
Seeking wonder in solitude, forever unpaired, I'm found.

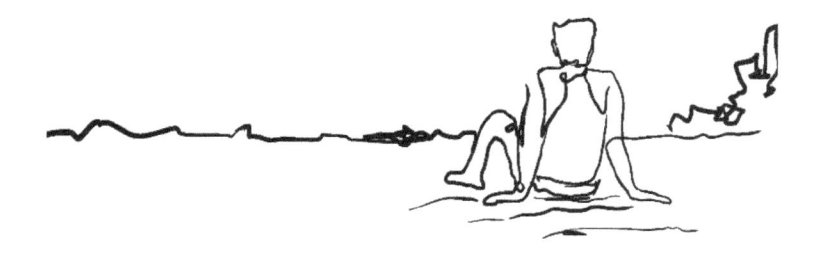

89.

Moments are passing by fast and inexperienced
Try to read my eyes and dive inside them.
I've forgiven and I'm letting it go
I told my heart.
Try and read those things which you are avoiding
I know you are not strong and are bound by the technicality of mind
Yet we both trust you
Or at least I try to.

90.

I'm so amazed by the waviness of the grass,
The emptiness it holds in the breeze.
No matter how fiercely the wind may blow,
It dances, unaffected by its gentle tease.

Perhaps it avoids something undisclosed,
Preferring detachment from its surroundings.
Trying not to get diverted by the love of a plant
Or a flower. But why? they asked.

It remains silent, never offering a reply,
Unperturbed by the questions that arise.
It made a choice to shatter the chains,
Opting to depart from the realm of chaos.

91.

One of the very first questions
I always ask myself
Every morning
Every day.
While others tries to grasp
I just watch it
Go through my skin from one end to the other
What should be taken care of?
Soul or body?
One feeds itself from the sunlight
One just enjoys the warmth of it
One will die one day
One will live every day.

Note to Myself

Printed in the USA
CPSIA information can be obtained
at www.ICGtesting.com
LVHW090635121124
796321LV00006B/129